Copycat Recipes Restaurant

Uncover the Secret Recipes of Your Favorite Restaurants and Make Tasty Dishes At Home By Following This Complete Compilation of Step-by-Step Recipes

GORDON RIPERT

Copyright © 2021 GORDON RIPERT

All rights reserved.

The content contained within this book may not be reproduced, duplicated or transmitted without direct written permission from the author or the publisher.

Under no circumstances will any blame or legal responsibility be held against the publisher, or author, for any damages, reparation, or monetary loss due to the information contained within this book, either directly or indirectly.

Legal Notice:
This book is copyright protected. It is only for personal use. You cannot amend, distribute, sell, use, quote or paraphrase any part, or the content within this book, without the consent of the author or publisher.

Disclaimer Notice:
Please note the information contained within this document is for educational and entertainment purposes only. All effort has been executed to present accurate, up to date, reliable, complete information. No warranties of any kind are declared or implied. Readers acknowledge that the author is not engaged in the rendering of legal, financial, medical or professional advice. The content within this book has been derived from various sources. Please consult a licensed professional before attempting any techniques outlined in this book.

By reading this document, the reader agrees that under no circumstances is the author responsible for any losses, direct or indirect, that are incurred as a result of the use of the information contained within this document, including, but not limited to, errors, omissions, or inaccuracies.

Sommario

INTRODUCTION 7

CHAPTER 1: COPYCAT BREAKFAST AND APPETIZER RECIPES FROM THE FAMOUS EATERIES 11
   1.1 COPYCAT BREAKFAST RECIPES 11
      Recipe 1 - Cinnamon Rolls- Copycat recipe from Cinnabon 11
      Recipe 2 - IHOP French toast Recipe (Copycat) 15
      Recipe 3 - Cracker Barrel Hash brown Casserole 17
      Recipe 4 - Starbucks Vanilla Bean Scones 19
      Recipe 5 - Bob Evan's Country Biscuit Breakfast 22
   1.2 COPYCAT APPETIZER RECIPES 25
      Recipe 1 - Texas Roadhouse Rattlesnake Bites 25
      Recipe 2 - Outback Steak's House Blooming Onion Petals 27
      Recipe 3 - Avocado Egg Rolls from Cheesecake Factory 29
      Recipe 4 - Fried Mozzarella sticks (Copycat from TGI Friday's) 31

CHAPTER 2: COPYCAT LUNCH AND DINNER RECIPES 34
   2.1 REPLICATED LUNCH RECIPES 34
      Recipe 1 - Panera's Mac and Cheese 34
      Recipe 2 - Gordon Ramsey's Salmon with Shellfish 38
      Recipe 3- PF Chang's Hot and Sour Soup 42
      Recipe 4 - Thai Green Coconut Curry (Pei Wei inspired) 44
      Recipe 5 - Copycat Subway Italian Hero 46
   2.2 COPYCAT DINNER RECIPES 49
      Recipe 1 - Copycat's McDonald's Fillet-O-Fish 49
      Recipe 2 - Vegan KFC Bowl 51
      Recipe 3 - Cracker Barrel's Meatloaf (copycat) 55
      Recipe 4 - Shake Shack Sloppy Joes (Copycat) 57
      Recipe 5 - Olive Garden's Alfredo Fettuccine 60

CHAPTER 3: COPYCAT RECIPES- SIDE DISHES, SALADS AND DRINKS 63
   3.1 COPYCAT RECIPES FOR SIDE DISHES 63
      Recipe 1 - Copycat Cilantro Lime Rice from Chipotle 63
      Recipe 2 - Copycat Longhorn Steakhouse Wild West Shrimp 67
      Recipe 3 - Rudy's Creamed Corns 69
      Recipe 4 - Chili's Black Beans 70

3.2 COPYCAT SALAD RECIPES 72
   Recipe 1 - Applebee's Oriental Chicken Salad............................ 72
   Recipe 2 - Mediterranean Kale Salad-copycat from Panera Bread.............. 74
3.3 COPYCAT DRINK RECIPES.. 77
   Recipe 1 - Chick-Fil-A Frosted Lemonade (copycat) 77
   Recipe 2 - Starbuck's Pumpkin Spice Latte... 79
   Recipe 3 - Mocha Frappe McDonald's... 81

CHAPTER 4: HAMBURGERS AND DESSERTS.................................. 85

4.1 COPYCAT HAMBURGER RECIPES 85
   Recipe 1 - Burger King Whooper.. 85
   Recipe 2 - Burger King-BK Big Fish Copycat 88
   Recipe 3 - Copycat McDonald's Big Mac 90
4.2 COPYCAT DESSERT RECIPES.. 92
   Recipe 1 - Cracker Barrel Coca Cola Cake... 92
   Recipe 2 - Trader Joe's Gone Bananas..................................... 94
   Recipe 3 - Ben and Jerry's Cherry Garcia Ice cream 96

CHAPTER 5: SPECIAL BONUS ARTISAN BREAD 98

5.1 ARTISAN BREAD RECIPES 98
   Recipe 1 - No-Knead Crusty Artisan Bread 98
   Recipe 2- Four ingredient easy Artisan Bread....................................... 101

CONCLUSION.. 103

Introduction

Many copycat meals can be made in under 30 minutes. And if you are considering a more complicated meal, you can always prepare in bulk and eat or freeze the surplus later in the week. Many commercially made foods are high in fat, salt, and sugar. When one cooks their own food, they know exactly which ingredients are going into the food and how much of each is going into it. Hence, people are in charge when they cook at home. There are 19 ingredients in McDonald's fries, for instance. One can make them even with lesser ingredients at home-and they are going to taste just as pleasant. Copycat recipes can be especially helpful if you or a family member has a food allergy. You could reduce the risk of an allergic reaction since you are in charge of your kitchen. One fantastic benefit of copycat recipes has the option to control one's portion of food. Many restaurants and quick-food joints provide much larger portions than are required. And the thing is, if food is in front of you, you will be eating it. You could limit the amount of food served for the dinner when you dine in, reducing excessive temptation. Preparing and eating such recipes at home offers opportunities for the whole family to chat about their day. It is not only a fun thing to do, but it is also a perfect way to teach your kids good eating habits by involving them in food preparation (maybe by letting them read the recipe out loud or mixing the ingredients). This cookbook has found and produced copycat recipes that beat the deal. Anyone can easily replicate these recipes at home without being an expert. These are the breakfast, appetizer, lunch, and dinner recipes, along with those for the side dishes, desserts, and salads from famous restaurants such as McDonald's, Cheesecake Factory, Subway, Krispy Kreme and Taco Bell. You would be able to find what makes those Glazed Cinnamon Doughnuts from the Krispy Kreme so delicious and why the Applebee's Hand-Battered Fish and Chips taste the way they do!

The table image below might help explain the conversion from metric (Europe) to US Standard Measurements while preparing the dishes. In case of weight, you will need to use the division sign to go from grams to the Standard US measurements.

Quick Alternatives		Capacity (US to metric)	
1 tablespoon (tbsp)	3 teaspoons (tsp)	1/5 teaspoon	1 milliliter
1/16 cup	1 tablespoon	1 teaspoon	5 milliliter
1/8 cup	2 tablespoons	1 tablespoon	15 milliliter

1/6 cup	2 tablespoons + 2 teaspoons	1 fluid oz	30 ml
1/4 cup	4 tablespoons	1/5 cup	47 ml
1/3 cup	5 tablespoons + 1 teaspoon	1 cup	237 ml
3/8 cup	6 tablespoons	2 cups (1 pint)	473 ml
1/2 cup	8 tablespoons	4 cups (1 quart)	0.95 liter
2/3 cup	10 tablespoons + 2 teaspoons	4 quarts (1 gal.)	3.8 liters
3/4 cup	12 tablespoons	**Weight (US to Metric)**	
1 cup	48 teaspoons	1 oz	28 grams
1 cup	16 tablespoons	1 pound	454 grams

8 fluid ounces (fl oz)	
1 pint (pt.)	2 cups
1 quart	2 pints

4 cups	1 quart
1 gallon	4 quarts
16 ounces	1 pound
1 milliliter	1 cubic centimeter
1 inch	2.54 centimeters

The following table might help with the temperatures.

Temperature Equivalents

500 F = 260 C
475 F = 245 C
450 F = 235 C
425 F = 220 C
400 F = 205 C
375 F = 190 C
350 F = 180 C
325 F = 160 C
300 F = 150 C
275 F = 135 C
250 F = 120 C
225 F = 107 C

*The nutrition information provided with each recipe inside the book is estimated and will differ according to the cooking methods and the product brands used.

Chapter 1: Copycat Breakfast and Appetizer Recipes from the Famous Eateries

1.1 Copycat Breakfast Recipes

Recipe 1 - Cinnamon Rolls- Copycat recipe from Cinnabon

Prep Time 30 minutes
Cook Time 20 minutes

Additional Time 1 hour
Total Time 1 hour 50 minutes

Ingredients

Cinnabon Dough Ingredients
1 (1/4 ounce) pack of active dry yeast
1 cup of hot milk
1/2 cup of granulated sugar
1/3 cup of melted butter
1 tsp of salt
Two eggs
4 cup of flour

Cinnamon rolls filling ingredients
1 cup of brown sugar
3 tbsp cinnamon
1/3 cup softened butter

Cinnabon Icing Ingredients (this recipe can be doubled if you want more icing!)
6 cup butter
1 1/2 cups of sugar powdered
1/4 cup cream cheese
1/2 cup vanilla
1/8 cup salt

Instructions for Cinnamon Rolls Recipe
- Dissolve the yeast in a large bowl of warm milk.
- Add sugar, butter, salt, eggs, and flour in a separate cup, then combine well.

- Place the mixture of milk/yeast into the pot, then mix. You'll need to get help from the dough hook if you are using a stand mixer. Mix thoroughly until well incorporated.
- Place the dough in a greased utensil, cover, and let it rise for around 1 hour in a warm place or until the dough has doubled in size.
- Roll out the dough on a silicon mat or floured surface until it is around 16-18 inches wide by 12 inches. It should be about 1/4 centimeter thick.

Make Copycat Cinnabon Filling and fill in the Cinnamon Rolls.
- Incorporate the butter, brown sugar, and cinnamon in a bowl to make the cinnamon filling.
- Spread the blend uniformly over the dough surface. You should spread the butter on the dough first, and then the brown sugar and cinnamon mixture if you prefer.

Back To Make the Best Cinnamon Homemade Rolls
- Beginning carefully from the long edge, roll down the dough to the bottom corner. The length of the roll should be about 18 inches. Break this roll into slices of 1 1/2 inches.
- Place the cut rolls in a 13-inch oiled pan. Cover them with a damp towel. Let them take another 30 minutes to grow before they double in size.
- Heat the oven to a temperature of 350 degrees, and bake until golden brown for 20 minutes.
- When the rolls are baking, mix all icing ingredients and beat well with an electric mixer until fluffy.

Notes
- Making fresh cinnamon rolls can be time-consuming, and you do not want to get up early in the day time so you can get them ready for breakfast. Instead, you can make these the night before and just let them rise in the morning for the second time, and bake.
- Just make this recipe up to the point that your rolls are cut and put in the oven. When cut and placed in the oven, instead of making them rise, cover them up and place them in the refrigerator.
- Take them out in the morning, allow them to rise for a second time, then bake as directed. (Please remember that it will take them a little longer to rise because they are cold from being in the refrigerator. Enable rising for 15-30 minutes longer.)

Nutrients: 880 calories, 36 grams of fat and 59 grams of sugar, the equivalent of 15 teaspoons

Recipe 2 - IHOP French toast Recipe (Copycat)

Servings 6 servings
Prep time 20 minutes
Cooking time 20 minutes

Ingredients
Two big eggs
1/2 cup 2 percent or homogenized milk
1.5 teaspoon of vanilla extract
Three tablespoons of all-purpose flour
Six slices of thick-cut French bread
Splash of table salt
Two tablespoons of salted butter
One tablespoon sugar

Optional ingredients
100 percent pure maple syrup
Sliced banana
Sliced strawberries

Walnuts
Pecans
Cinnamon
Whipped cream

Instructions

- The eggs, milk, vanilla extract, and all-purpose flour are to be mixed in a medium mixing bowl. Whisk together until the batter is smooth, even, and start bubbling slightly.
- Add the butter and heat at medium in a frying pan until the butter is melted and starts sizzling slightly (about 1-2 minutes).
- In the meantime, dip one slice of French bread into the mixture of the eggs and submerge until the whole slice is thoroughly soaked. Remove from the mixing bowl and place it onto the hot frying pan.
- Cook by the side for 2-3 minutes, or until golden brown.
- Repeat the cycle with the rest of the bread slices.
- Serve with optional ingredients on top: maple syrup, sliced banana, sliced strawberries, sugar, salt, chopped walnuts or pecans, cinnamon, and whipped cream.

Calories: 230 kcal; approximately: Fat: 16.00g, Carbs: 23.00g, Protein: 13.00g

Recipe 3 - Cracker Barrel Hash brown Casserole

Much like the original Cracker Barrel version, this Hash brown Casserole is easy to throw together and serve with breakfast, or even dinner. (Plus, freezer-friendly leftovers!)

Prep time: 5 minutes
Cook time: 45 minutes
Resting time: 10 minutes
Total time: 50 minutes
Servings: 8

Ingredients
32 oz. Frozen hash browns, thawed *
One and a half cup of chocolate, melted
10.5 oz. Chicken soup cream, (cheddar cream works too)
16 oz. sour cream
One small, finely diced onion

2 Cups of cheddar cheese, grated
1/3 cup of pepper

Directions
- Preheat the oven to 350 ° C.
- Make sure your hash browns are thawed. (They take too long a time to bake otherwise.) You can unfreeze them in the microwave to accelerate this process.
- Pat them so that excess water can be removed.
- Set aside 1/2 cup of cheddar cheese.
- In a large utensil, add all of the remaining ingredients.
- Place it in a 9x13 casserole oiled dish and top with the remaining cheese.
- Bake, uncovered, for 35 minutes.
- Raise the temperature to 375 degrees and bake for another 10 minutes, until the top begins to be slightly crisp and brown.
- Take out from the oven and let sit for 10 minutes, then serve!

Note
- You can also use frozen Cubed Hash Browns.

Make-ahead process

This recipe can be prepared one night before and frozen overnight in the fridge, just be sure the hash browns are thawed and patted dry before you mix them with the other ingredients.

Storing the remainders

The residuals should be refrigerated in an airtight jar and are best by using 25 minutes or more based on the size of the portion.

Leftovers can also be frozen; they're better if used within three months. To heat again, let it defrost in the refrigerator and bake it sealed at 350 ° oven for about 25-30 minutes.

Nutrition

Calories: 664 kcal, Carbohydrates: 45g, Protein: 12g, Fat: 48g, Saturated Fat: 22g, Cholesterol: 92mg, Sodium: 971mg, Potassium: 799mg, Fiber: 3g, Sugar: 4g, Vitamin A: 1060IU, Vitamin C: 16.3mg, Calcium: 294mg, Iron: 1.3mg

Recipe 4 - Starbucks Vanilla Bean Scones

Starbucks' popular mini vanilla bean scones go keto and free of sugar. Take a cup of coffee and enjoy a healthy breakfast treat.

Prep Time 10 mins
Cook Time 18 mins
Total Time 28 mins

Servings: 12 Portions
Calories: 202 kcal

Ingredients

Scones
3 Cups almond flour
1/3 tablespoon Sweetener
1 Tbsp of Baking Powder
1 Tsp vanilla powder or seeds scraped from 1 vanilla bean or 1 tsp vanilla extract
1/4 tsp salt
Two large eggs
1/4 cup butter, melted
2 cups of heavy cream
1/2 tsp Vanilla Extract

Glaze
Powdered 1/2-cup Swerve Sweetener
1/2 tsp vanilla powder or 1/2 tsp vanilla bean seeds or 1/2 tsp vanilla extract
1/4 cup cream, heavy
Water if you have too thick a glaze

Instructions

Scones
- Preheat oven temperature to 325F and line a large parchment or silicone liner baking sheet.
- Whisk the almond flour, the sweetener, baking powder, vanilla powder, and salt together in a large bowl.

- Stir in the eggs; butter melted, milk, and vanilla extract until the dough is mixed.
- Cut the dough into three even parts and form into disks, each about 1 inch thick and between 5 and 6 inches in diameter. Cut each disc into eight similar pieces.
- Place on a prepared baking sheet and bake for 15 to 18 minutes, or until the touch is just golden and firm.
- Remove, and let it cool.

Glaze
- Whisk Swerve, vanilla powder, and cream together in a medium bowl until well combined. If your glaze is thick, add one teaspoon of water at a time until it achieves a dippable consistency.
- Submerge the top of each scone into glaze and place, until set, on a baker's rack.

Nutrition Facts
Calories: 202
Fat: 17.34 g, Cholesterol: 41 mg, Carbs: 6.82g, Fiber: 3.09g, Protein: 7.24g

Recipe 5 - Bob Evan's Country Biscuit Breakfast

4 Servings
15 m Prep Time
15 m Cook Time
30 m Total time

Ingredients
4 Large biscuits (homemade or refrigerated type; prepared)
1 lb Sausage for Breakfast
4 Eggs, large
1 A cup of cheddar shredded cheese
2 1/2 cups of milk
Four tbsps. Flour
4 tbsps. Unsalted butter
1 tsp kosher salt
1/2 tsp black chili pepper

Directions

Step one
If not already made, prepare the biscuits.

Step two
Place brown sausage in a large skillet, which crumbles as it cooks and drains any fat.

Step 3
Melt butter in another large pan, and pour in flour.

Step 4
Heat flour, stirring, over low heat until it just starts changing color (it doesn't have to get dark/brown coffee color).

Step 5
Whisk in the milk, salt, and pepper and continue to stir until the mixture thickens.

Step 6
Include a little flour into a small amount of milk until smooth, if you like the gravy thickness, and whisk it into the gravy; if you like it thinner, just add more milk and stir until blended.

Step 7
In a small skillet, cook eggs alone, either sunny-side-up or over-easy, whichever you prefer (this is best when the yolk is still a bit runny).

Step 8
Divide the biscuit for each serving, and put on the tray.

Step 9

Complete with a crumbled sausage biscuit and fill with a fried egg.

Step 10

Sprinkle some cheddar cheese and coat the egg with milk gravy.

Step 11

If you like melty cheese, microwave for about 30-45 seconds.

Step 12

If needed, serve with hash browns or cheese grits.

Nutritional facts

Serving Size: 1 (430.3 g), Calories 1108.1, Total Fat - 73.8 g, Saturated Fat - 25.8 g, Cholesterol - 357.9 mg, Sodium - 2429.7 mg, Total Carbohydrate - 60 g, Dietary Fiber - 4.8 g Sugars - 3.6 g, Protein - 50.7 g, Calcium - 407.4 mg, Iron - 6.3 mg, Vitamin C - 9.1 mg, Thiamin - 1.1 mg

1.2 Copycat Appetizer Recipes

Recipe 1 - Texas Roadhouse Rattlesnake Bites

Yield: 36 bites
Prep Time: 15 minutes
Cook Time: 20 minutes
Total Time: 1 hour 5 minutes

Ingredients
2 Cups of cheese (Monterey Jack), shredded
2 Jalapeños, chopped
1 Clove of garlic, chopped
1 Cup flour
1 Large beaten egg

1 Cup of milk
1 1/2 cups of crumbs of plain bread
1 tsp. paprika
One tsp. of garlic powder
Cayenne pepper one teaspoon
Vegetable oil or canola, to fry

Directions
- In a bowl, combine your shredded cheese and jalapenos and mix together.
- Shape the cheese mixture into roughly 3/4 inch balls, pressing tightly for compression.
- Put the balls on the thin cookie sheet and freeze for a minimum of 60 minutes but preferably for 2 hours.
- Preheat the deep fryer until 350 degrees.
- Place the flour in a bowl.
- In a second container, mix the egg and milk together.
- In a third utensil, bring together the bread crumbs, paprika, garlic powder, and cayenne pepper.
- Roll the chilled balls in the mixture of flour, dip into the mix of eggs, and finally coat it with the mix of bread crumbs.
- Fry between 3-4 minutes in a pan, or until golden brown.
- Drain onto a towel of paper.
- Serve with your favorite sauces to dip in.

Nutrition Facts

Yield: 36 bites, amount per serving: 86 calories, Calories: 86 g, Carbohydrate: 9 g, Protein: 3 g, Fat: 4 g, Fats (saturated): 2 g, Cholesterol: 12 mg, Sodium: 72 mg, Potassium: 37 mg, Fiber: 1 g, Sugar: 1 g, Vitamin A: 127 g, Vitamin C: 1 g, Calcium: 65 g, Iron: 1 g

Recipe 2 - Outback Steak's House Blooming Onion Petals

Prep Time 15 mins
Cook Time 10 mins
Total Time 25 mins
Servings: 12 approx.

Ingredients

Wet mixture
One medium-sized egg
½ cup milk

Dry Mixture
1 Cup flour
1 1/2 teaspoon paprika
1 tsp. salt
1 Tsp of cayenne chili
1/2 tsp black chili
1/2 tsp powdered garlic
Oregano 1 1/2 Tsp.
1 1/2 tsp. cumin
3-4 Onions, small
4-6 cups of veg. oil or other edible oil

Directions
- In a medium-sized container, add all of your wet ingredients.
- In a small, shallow utensil, mix all your dry ingredients.
- Slice your onions to the ends, then cut them in half. Slice the onions into petals of 1 inch, and set aside.
- In a wide frying pot, add oil and heat for around 5 minutes over medium heat, or until hot and slightly ripple.
- Dip into the wet batter to coat the onions, then the dry batter, then back into the wet batter and dry mixture again. Place all petals aside and repeat.
- Place them into the heated oil and fry for 3-4 minutes, then turn them over carefully if necessary. Remove from oil and put on a lined sheet of paper towel.

- Repeat this on all of the onions.
- Serve right away with Bloom Sauce.

Nutrition
Calories: 117kcal, Carbohydrates: 22g, Protein: 4g, Fat: 1g, Cholesterol: 27mg, Sodium: 20mg, Potassium: 86mg, Sugar: 1g, Vitamin A: 95IU, Vitamin C: 0.7mg, Calcium: 40mg, Iron: 1.5mg

Recipe 3 - Avocado Egg Rolls from Cheesecake Factory

Prep Time 15 minutes
Cook Time 3 minutes
Total Time 18 minutes
Servings 3 Egg Rolls
Calories 439 kcal

Ingredients

3 Wrappers of Egg Roll
3 Big Avocados
3 Tbsp Sun-dried tomatoes lined with oil
3 Tsp minced Cilantro
1 Tsp garlic salt
1 Egg

Dip sauce
1/4 tsp Vinegar, White
Balsamic Vinegar 1 Tsp
Honey 1/2 Cup
One pinch Saffron Powdered
1/2 cup Shredded Cashews
2/3 cup cilantro
2 Garlic Cloves
1 tbsp Sugar
1 Tsp Chili pepper
1 tsp Cumin
Olive oil: 1/4 cup

Directions
- Stir the vinegar, honey, and saffron together in a pot. Heat up in the microwave for 1 minute.
- Puree this mixture, adding cashews, 2/3 cup cilantro, garlic, sugar, pepper, and cumin in a blender. Add the oil and pour it into a container. Remove and add to the fridge.
- Stir avocado, tomatoes, 1 tsp, together in a bowl: cilantro, and some salt. Add half of the mixture to the mid of each wrapper of the egg roll.

- Place the wrapper, such that the corner points to you. Fold over the bottom corner. Fold remaining edges over the filling and brush with an egg to keep the corners in place. Roll up from the bottom and fold the top corner over it. Seal the remaining wraps with egg and repeat.
- Fry rolling of the eggs for 3-5 minutes or until golden brown.
- Serve with sauce to dip in.

Nutritional Facts
Fat 22g 34%, Saturated Fat 3g 19%, Cholesterol 55mg 18%, Sodium 884mg 38%, Potassium 311mg 9%, Carbohydrates 60g 20%, Fiber 1g 4%, Sugar 50g 56%, Protein 3g 6%

Recipe 4 - Fried Mozzarella sticks (Copycat from TGI Friday's)

Prep Time: 10 minutes
Cook Time: 10 minutes
Total Time: 20 minutes

Servings: 4
Calories: 751 kcal

Ingredients
1 Lb Mozzarella Cheese
1 Cup flour
1/4 cup cornstarch
2 Cups Seasoned Italian breadcrumbs
1 Cup of milk
Vegetable cooking oil

Directions
- Cut cheese sticks into roughly 3/8 inch thick, long slices. In a pot, add the flour and the cornstarch. Drop the cheese plank into the flour, then dip the cheese stick into the breadcrumbs after soaking into a bowl of whole milk.
- Shake off excess breadcrumbs and put the stick of mozzarella on a wire rack. Scrap the flour. Repeat until all sticks of cheese have been dipped.
- After all the cheese sticks have been submerged, put them back in milk, then for the second time in bread crumbs, and shake off the bits of bread.
- For frying, preheat vegetable oil to 350. Drop the cheese into hot oil and fry until golden brown. This will take no longer than 1 minute. Remove the cheese stick from the oil and place it to cool on a wire rack. Serve with the marinara sauce you like.

Macro-nutrients

Calories: 751kcal Carbohydrate: 77 g Protein: 38 g Fat: 30 g Saturated fat: 16 g Cholesterol: 96 mg Sodium: 1540 mg Potassium: 338 mg Fiber: 3 g Sugar: 7 g Vitamin A: 980IU Vitamin C: 1.7 mg Calcium: 755 mg Iron: 4.9 mg Vitamin A: 980IU Vitamin C: 1.7 mg Vitamin C: 7555 mg

Chapter 2: Copycat Lunch and Dinner Recipes

2.1 Replicated Lunch Recipes

Recipe 1 - Panera's Mac and Cheese

Prep time 15 mins
Cook time 20 mins
Total time 35 mins

Ingredients
1 lb Shells of medium pasta, or elbow macaroni

Roux
Butter ½ cup
Flour ½ cup

Cheddar White Sauce
Cracker Barrel Vermont White Cheddar: 3 1/2 cups shredded, one block = 2 cups
3 tbsp. flour
Half and half 2.5 ups
1.5 cups of milk, better to be whole

Flavorings
Salt ½ tsp.
Chili pepper ½ tsp.
1 Tablespoon Mustard
One tsp. of onion powder
Hot sauce 2 tbsp.

Instructions

Shred the Cheese
Grate the cheese initially and place aside. It should be near room temperature when applied to the sauce. Sprinkle with three tablespoons flour and swirl to cover.

Boil the Pasta
Boil water in a large utensil and cook according to pasta box instructions. Drain well when done. Prepare the sauce as the water boils and the pasta cooks.

Prepare the Sauce
- Pro hack: Measure out all of your cooking materials and get them ready when you cook the sauce.
- Microwave the milk in three 30-second intervals, mixing in between.
- Melt the butter in a utensil over medium heat. Put in the flour for 1 minute, until it begins to take a mild golden color.
- Slowly place in the half and half and milk and whisk. Whisk for around 3 minutes.
- Stir in the seasonings and hot sauce.
- Reduce the heat to moderate. Sprinkle slowly in the shredded cheese, stirring as you do.
- Continuously whisk and thicken until smooth. Take off heat.
- Use cooked pasta to mix and stir. Service!

In case you baked
- Simmer the pasta for 1 minute less than al dente.
- Transfer to a lightly greased 9 x 13-inch saucepan. (Optional: 1 cup of crushed Ritz crackers on top.)
- Bake for 15 minutes, at 325 degrees.
- Let it rest for five minutes before consuming it.

Notes

Method: Crock Pot
For 5 minutes, cook the pasta shells or the elbow macaroni, not more than that.
Follow the rest, as illustrated in the instructions.

Transfer to a lightly greased Crock-Pot and cook for 2-3 hours at low or 1-2 at high.

Note: Crockpots differ in how much heat they give off. So check it regularly and turn it to warm up until ready to serve, if necessary.

Various options for cheese
Feel free to modify this recipe to add various flavors, using as many cheeses as you like!

Gouda
Mozzarella
Light Cheddar
Monterey Jack
Gruyere

The Hot Sauce
The Hot Sauce is used solely to improve cheese flavor.
Adding hot sauce to macaroni and cheese may sound shocking, particularly if you plan on serving this to children. But this doesn't make the recipe hot at all, and you can't taste it at all.

Nutrition
Calories: 645 kcal, Carbohydrate: 56 g, Protein: 25 g, Fat: 35 g, Saturated Fat: 22 g, Cholesterol: 103 mg, Sodium: 695 mg, Potassium: 348 mg, Fiber: 2 g, Sugar: 7 g, Vitamin A: 1105IU, Vitamin C: 3 mg, Calcium: 507 mg, Iron: 2 mg

Recipe 2 - Gordon Ramsey's Salmon with Shellfish

Servings 4
Time for prep 40 min
Cooking Time 30 min
Total Time 1 hr. 10 min

Ingredients

For the broth
Mussels 10 oz
Littleneck clams of 10 oz
2 tbsp. of extra virgin olive oil
One celery, diced
1 Carrot, diced and peeled
1 Shallot, cut roughly
One sprig lemon thyme
One lemon
Seasonal salt

1 1/2 cups of dry white wine (Sauvignon Blanc, for example)
2 Cups of chicken stock unsalted
Fronds of Fennel

For Pasta and Vegetables
1 Tiny zucchini, 1/4 "bits diced
1 Little fennel with fronds, split into 1/4 "pieces, reserve the fronds.
2/3 cup of fresh, or frozen and thawed English peas
2/3 Cup white canned beans, rinsed and drained
1/2 cup elbow macaroni (Gluten-free tip: many wheat-free kinds of pasta are available in most grocers and online).

The Salmon
4 (4.5-5 oz) center-cut salmon filets, deboned, skin on
Seasonal salt
Black pepper, freshly ground
Two tbsp. of extra virgin olive oil and some more to drizzle

Tips to Break a Whole Salmon
- To break down a whole salmon, Chef Ramsay provides the following advice:
- Test to see if no scales are left. Brush the skin back with the tip of your knife, from head to tail. This will make the strokes of the knife more secure.
- Wipe your knife off each time you cut it into the Salmon. A clean knife makes a clean cut.
- The higher you step up into the Salmon's belly while making portions of your filet, the thinner you slice.

How to make the Broth for Shellfish?

- Scrub the clams and mussels well under cold, running water for 10 minutes, draining as required. Remove beards from the mussels and discard any free shells. Deposit aside. Heat the oil over medium to high heat in a big pan. Add the mirepoix (carrot, celery, and shallot), thyme, and one slice of lemon while saving the rest of the lemon for later use — season for 30 seconds, with salt and sweat. Add the shellfish and place a cap over the bowl — Cook for about 30 seconds. Include the wine, then cover and cook for another 30 seconds.

- Pour in the stock of chicken, cover and heat up to high, cooking for 5-7 minutes before the shellfish opens. Strain the broth into a saucepan and pour the broth into a clean bowl. Drop the shellfish into a bowl, discard any shells that have not opened. Deposit aside.

How to make Pasta and Vegetables?
- Place a medium-sized pot of salted water over high heat to boil. Take 2 minutes to blanch the vegetables. Quickly extract the vegetables from under cold water with a hand-sieve or slotted spoon and rinse. Drain in a tub, and hold. Stir the beans into the vegetables. Add the pasta and cook in the pot of boiling water for 7-8 minutes until just al dente.
- Squeeze the pasta into a colander, rinse with cold water to avoid the cooking, and extract the starch. Add the pasta to the beans and vegetables.

How to prepare the Salmon

- Pull the Salmon skin off a little. Season with salt on both sides, and black pepper, freshly ground. Heat a large non-adhesive pan over medium-high heat. Stir in the olive oil and put the Salmon gently into the pan, skin-side down. Cook for 6-7 minutes and transform on occasion. Remove the fish to rest on a platter while the soup is being prepared.

Serving
- Return the shellfish broth pot to a boil over medium to high heat — lower the temperature to a simmer. Include the reserved fennel fronds and lemon zest. Add the shellfish, potatoes, beans, and pasta and gently cook, just to warm up — flavor with salt and a bit of lemon juice as per taste. Ladle the minestrone to a bowl's middle. Place the Salmon on top, skin upside, and dribble some olive oil.

General information about the macro-nutrients (depending upon what size of Salmon you take)
Calories 419.9, Total Fat 16.1 g, Saturated Fat 5.6 g, Polyunsaturated Fat 2.6 g, Monounsaturated Fat 4.8 g, Cholesterol 100.4 mg, Sodium 1,376.2 mg, Potassium 1,277.7 mg, Total Carbohydrate 28.0 g, Dietary Fiber 4.8 g, Sugars 2.5 g, Protein 36.5 g

Recipe 3- PF Chang's Hot and Sour Soup

Prep + cooking time 25 mins
Servings 4-6
Yield 6 cups

Ingredients
Chicken breasts, cut into narrow strips, 6 ounces
Chicken stock 1 quart
Soy Sauce 1 cup
1 Teaspoon white pepper
6 oz. Bamboo sticks, cut into pieces (canned would be preferred)
6 Ounces wood ear mushrooms, sliced into strips (or canned straw mushrooms, if you cannot find wood ear)
1/2 cup Cornstarch
Water 1/2 cup
Two beaten Eggs
4 ounces white vinegar
6 ounces tofu, sliced into strips

Directions
- Cook strips of chicken till cooked. Deposit back.
- Put stock to simmer. Add the soy sauce, white pepper, bamboo, chicken, and mushrooms. Stir. Let them cook for about 3 minutes.
- When cooking, add cornstarch and water to form a slurry, in a separate bowl. Add a little slurry at a time and mix until thick (any slurry might not be enough, so add as much as possible for the desired thickness- around 3/4 of the slurry can be used).
- Add eggs and cook for 30 seconds while stirring, or until the eggs are cooked.
- Switch the heat off. Add tofu and vinegar, and give it a little swirl. Spoon in and enjoy!

Nutritional Facts

Calories 470, Calories from Fat 110, fats 12g, saturated fats 2.5g, trans fats 0g, Cholesterol 185mg, Sodium 3800mg, carbs 63g, dietary fiber 3g, sugar 8g, protein 26g

Recipe 4 - Thai Green Coconut Curry (Pei Wei inspired)

4 Servings
Prep time: 15 mins
Cook time: 15 mins
Total time: 30 mins

Ingredients
2 Pounds of coconut oil
Two medium-breasts of chicken (cut into bits of 1 ½ inch)
¼ tsp. salt
1/4 tsp. chili pepper
1 Tablespoon of garlic, finely minced

1/4 lb. Green beans (cleaned, in 2 parts cut)
1/2 red bell pepper (chopped into cubes of 1 inch)
1/2 green bell pepper (chopped into cubes of 1 inch)
2 Carrots (cut in circles of ½ inch)
1 Small onion (cut into cubes of 1 inch)
One can coconut milk
3 tbsp. Green Curry Paste
1 Tablespoon ginger root, finely chopped
One lime zest
1/2 lime juice
2 Thai dried red chilies (see note)
2 Spoonfuls of soft brown sugar
Turmeric ¼ tsp.
(Optional) 1 Pinch red pepper flakes
8–10 basil leaves, half cut

Directions
- Heat up the oil in a sauté pan on medium-low heat. Drop in the chicken, garlic, salt, and pepper and cook for approximately 4 minutes or until just cooked. Put the chicken on a plate and keep warm.
- Apply the remaining oil to the green beans and sauté for about 3 minutes. Shift to plate. Next, just sauté the peppers, onions, and carrots together for 1 minute. Where appropriate, add a few extra drops of oil in between. Transfer the green beans to the same plate.
- Put the coconut milk, green curry paste, ginger root, lime zest, lime juice, dried Thai chilies, brown sugar of light color, turmeric, and red pepper flakes into the same sauté pan. Take all of that to simmer lightly. Continue cooking until the curry shrinks to about half. Add the

chicken and all the vegetables back into the same pot and heat all through the way. Sprinkle with leafy basil. With jasmine rice, serve warm!

Note
Depending on your choice for spice, the dried Thai red peppers may be omitted. Cut off the tops and take out the seeds if you want to get some of the flavors. Without carrying too much heat, this will help to create the flavor.

Nutrition
Calories 380 kcals, Fats 19g, Carbs 23g, Protein 30g

Recipe 5 - Copycat Subway Italian Hero

Italian Hero Sub Sandwich is a copycat of the famous Subway, which makes lunch delicious and simple for the crowd!

Prep time 10 mins
Total time 10 mins
Servings 3

Ingredients
Deli hoagie buns 3
6 oz. variety pack of finely sliced Italian (Salami, Capocollo, and Calabrese) meats
Six sliced cheese, Provolone
Choice of spinach, lettuce, tomato, cabbage, pickles, and banana peppers, olives, etc.
Mayonnaise
Dijon Mustard

Directions
- Lengthwise slice the hoagie buns and top with the vegetables, Provolone, and meats.
- Dress each sandwich with Mayonnaise and Dijon when serving immediately, then cut in half.
- Wrap each sub in a cling wrap and store refrigerated for up to 48 hours, if served later.

Nutritional Values
480 calories, Fat 24 g, Carbs 46 g, Fiber 5 g, Protein 20 g

Some Side Notes
You can top up your sandwiches with whatever vegetables and dressings you want, just like when you are at Subway. Subway recommends dressing the sandwich up with olive oil and red vinegar.

Healthy Subway Sandwich
You could increase the fiber in your sub sandwich by opting for whole-grain wheat bread and make it healthier. You'll cut down on the fats by choosing lighter options such as a red wine vinaigrette and lean sandwich meats.
When you do these beforehand, hold off any dressing until they're served, so they're transported well. They're going to be kept that way best, and not get soggy.

Difference between a sub-sandwich and a sub
Sub sandwich is a sandwich made with a wise long bread roll, reminiscent of a submarine; it is a namesake. With a diverse range of meats, cheeses, vegetables, and dressings, they are piled high. Those Italian Hero Sub Sandwiches are the ideal lunch recipe when you're on a picnic. The meats provide so much spice and flavor, ideal for adults in need of a fast and easy portable lunch. They are perfect when you are not looking for a boring old ham and cheese sandwich. Give this yummy sub sandwich a try!

2.2 Copycat Dinner Recipes

Recipe 1 - Copycat's McDonald's Fillet-O-Fish

Prep Time 15 mins
Cook Time 20 mins
Total time roughly around 35 mins
Yield 4-6
Serving size one sandwich
Calories 470

Ingredients

Fish filets
2 Large fillets of Pollock, tilapia, cod or other white fish (about 1.25 pounds)
Lemon juice 2 tbsp.
1/2 cup of milk

Two finely ground cups of oyster or Saltine crackers
A half-cup of breadcrumbs
2 Cups cooking oil (peanut, canola, or vegetable)

For tartar sauce
2 Tablespoons of diced white onion
1/3 cup mayonnaise
2 Teaspoons of chopped dill pickles, with juice
Salt, a pinch

To serve
American cheese: 4–6 slices
4–6 White Buns, (those used for hamburgers)

Instructions
- Split the fillets into 3 "by 3" squares — Reserve scraps, too (waste not, don't want to!).
- Drop the fish in a shallow bowl and brush with the juice of lemons. Enable marinating to last for 10 minutes. Meanwhile, put crumbs with parchment or waxed paper in a shallow cup, and line a plate or baking sheet.
- Drain the excess lemon juice and to the fish some milk.
- Carefully bring the bits out and dredge them in crumbs to cover completely. Dip again with the butter, then crumbs for a strong coating. Place coated fillets onto the paper and refrigerate for up to 3 hours for 10 minutes to help apply the coating.
- Create the tartar sauce you want.
- Bring together the onions, pickles, and mayo with a tablespoon of salt and white pepper.
- Chill out in the refrigerator.

- Cut and unwrap cheese slices.
- In a large-sized cooking pot heat, 1/2 inch deep oil until a crumb sizzles when dropped in. It should have a temperature of about 350 F.
- Fry the fillets on each side, cold from the fridge, for about 2 minutes.
- Move fillets onto a rack when golden and cooked clean.
- Warm the buns up for 10 seconds or until soft in the microwave.
- Put a slice of cheese on the bottom of each bun, top with a square of fish or two for more enormous sandwiches, a huge scoop of tartar sauce, and each one immediately!
- This makes four large sandwiches or six smaller sandwiches.

Recipe 2 - Vegan KFC Bowl

In reality, vegan KFC bowls are better than the actual ones! This recipe for KFC bowls is made from crispy and spicy air-fried cauliflower bits, garlicky mashed potatoes, corn, and moist brown gravy toppings. Best bowl of mashed potatoes ever!

Two servings
Prep time 30 mins
Cook time 50 mins
Total time 1 hour 20 mins

Ingredients

Fried Cauliflower pieces
1 Medium Cauliflower Head
2 Eggcitables Eggs (or any egg sub)
Almond milk: 3/4 cup
1 Tsp Apple Cider Vinegar
Cup 3/4 Flour
Paprika 2 Tsp
1 Tsp Garlic Powder
1 Tsp of Powdered Onion
1 Tbsp Parsley Flakes
Oregano 1 Tsp.
Cinnamon: 1/2 tsp
1/2 tsp. Allspice
1/4 tsp nutmeg
Marjoram 1 Tsp.
Sugar 1 Tsp
Salt 2 tsp
Pepper 2 tsp

Mashed garlic potatoes
5 Little Red Potatoes
1 Tbsp Butter
Almond milk: 1/2 cup
2 Tsp Garlic Powder
Parsley flakes 1 Tbsp
2 tsp Salt
2 Tsp Pepper

Vegan Bowl of KFC
1 1/2 cups Mashed Potatoes with garlic
1 1/2 cups Bits of cauliflower
1/2 Cup Corn Niblets
1 Cup Vegan Gravy (brown gravy used in this recipe)

Directions

Bites of a Fried Cauliflower
- Wash a cauliflower head and cut it into little bits of bite-size. Deposit back.
- Combine the Eggcitables egg, almond milk, and apple cider vinegar in a mixing bowl.
- Combine flour and seasonings in yet another mixing bowl.
- Put the cauliflower in the wet mixture, a few pieces at a time, and toss to coat.
- When covered in the wet mixture, throw the cauliflower into the dry flour mixture until it is evenly coated. Set aside in a separate bowl, or directly in the basket of the air fryer.

- At medium heat, fry the cauliflower in the air fryer for about 25 - 30 minutes, regularly flipping to ensure even cooking. At the end of the cooking, turn heat to the extreme to make the cauliflower extra crispy.

Mashed garlic potatoes
- Place a saucepan of salted water to boil.
- Wash the potatoes and peel, then cut them into small chunks.
- Broil the potatoes in water for about 15 minutes, or until profoundly tender. Then drain the potatoes into the pot and return them to the stovetop.
- Add the butter, almond milk, powdered garlic, parsley flakes, salt, and pepper. Press with a fork or potato masher until it reaches the desired consistency.

Vegan Bowl KFC
- Heat the corn nibbles over medium heat in a tiny frying pan. If desired season with salt and pepper.
- Add mashed potatoes, air-fried cauliflower, and corn niblets to a large, shallow bowl.
- Top the bowl with gravy flakes and more parsley.
- Treat yourself to the best KFC version ever!

Nutritional Information
Calories: 690, Fat: 31g, Carbs: 77g, Protein: 27g

Recipe 3 - Cracker Barrel's Meatloaf (copycat)

Cracker Barrel Meatloaf Copycat is delicious and can be easily made. It's the perfect comfort food, cracker meatloaf recipe, along with the best glaze!

Prep time 20 mins
Cooking time 50 mins
Total time 70 mins
Yield: 8

Ingredients

Meatloaves
1 1/2 lbs. (24 ounces) of ground beef, 80/20
Three large, beaten eggs
1 cup of Ritz crackers (crushed), around 1 1/2 sleeves

One small yellow onion, thinly diced
1/2 green, finely diced bell pepper (you can use red too)
3 cups of fresh cheddar cheese, shredded
One teaspoon of oregano, ground
One teaspoon of thyme, ground
One tsp. of garlic powder
Two tablespoons fresh, finely chopped parsley
Whole milk, ½ cup
Worcestershire sauce, 1 tbsp
1/2 teaspoon of salt
1/8 teaspoon black pepper

For the topping
A half-cup ketchup
Packed light brown sugar, 1/2 cup
Mustard, 1 tsp.
Apple cider vinegar, 1 tsp

Directions
- Preheat oven to 350 F.
- Add the minced beef to a large utensil and start slicing it into big crumbs using a spoon.
- Apply the remaining ingredients from the "Meatloaf" list to the ground beef and blend well to be cooked in full. You may use your hands to bring everything together.
- Cover an aluminum foil on a baking dish. Spray with some cooking spray on it to grease it. Transfer the beef mixture to the center of the baking platter and form into a loaf. Also, a 9x5 inch meatloaf pan can be used for the beef mixture.
- Bake the meatloaf for 30 minutes in a preheated oven.

- Meanwhile, add to a small bowl all the "topping" ingredients and stir to combine.
- Place the topping over the meatloaf and bake for another 20-30 minutes. Until the top is golden brown and until meatloaf is cooked at an internal temperature of 160 degrees F at the center.
- Get the loaf of meat from the oven and let it rest for 10 minutes before slicing.

Side Notes
- The best meatloaf recipes contain plenty of moisture from the best meat-to-fat ratio. 80/20- that is the best option. Anything leaner is going to turn your meatloaf dry.
- Use fresh cheese, which is shredded. In a pre-shredded cheese, the anti-caking ingredients will absorb the moisture in the meatloaf.
- In this recipe, green bell pepper is used, but if you're not a fan of it, you can use red or skip it altogether.

Nutrients
460 calories, Fats 27g, Carbs 33g, Fiber 4g, Protein 21 g

Recipe 4 - Shake Shack Sloppy Joes (Copycat)

Sloppy Joes from Shake Shack are made with a sauce from copycat Shake Shack. Your kids would love a messy burger packed with cheese on a potato bun.

Yield: 4 servings
Prep Time: 5 minutes
Cook Time: 8 minutes
Total Time: 13 minutes

Ingredients
1 1/2 pounds of beef, ground (85/15)
Kosher salt 1 tsp.
1/4 teaspoon black pepper, ground
Worcestershire sauce two teaspoons
Martin's Sandwich Potato Rolls 4
4 Lettuce leaves, green leaf
8 Tomato slices
4 Slices of American cheese
3/4 cup Shake Shack sauce, divided
Vegetable oil

Directions

- Brown your ground beef halfway, around 3-4 minutes, then mix in salt, pepper, and Worcestershire sauce in your large skillet.
- Cook the beef for around 3-4 minutes, until thoroughly browned.
- Switch off the heat then add the Shake Shack sauce in 1/2 cup.
- Serve with cheese, onion, lettuce, and leftover Shake Shack sauce.

Nutritional Data

Yield: 4 servings, amount per serving: 588 calories, Carbohydrates: 28 g, Proteins: 44 g, Fat: 34 g, Saturated Fat: 14 g, Cholesterol: 137 mg, Sodium: 1260 mg, Potassium: 710 mg, Fiber: 2 g, Sugar: 7 g, Vitamin A: 1722 g, Vitamin C: 9 g, Calcium: 409 g, Iron: 6 g.

Serve: The Shake Shack Sloppy Joes can be kept at room temperature for up to 2 hours.

Store: Keep your Sloppy Joes in an airtight jar in the refrigerator for three days.

Freeze: Cool meat in a sealed container absolutely before freezing for up to 3 months.

Variations

Shake Stack: Top with the fried mushrooms and Muenster cheese your Shake Shack Sloppy Joes to get the same flavor as the Shake Stack Burger.

Smoke Stack: Add Applewood Smoked Bacon and cherry peppers to make these Smoke Stack Sloppy Joes. In most grocery stores close to pickles and olives, you can pick the pickled cherry peppers, also called sweet peppers or piquante peppers.

Meat: 85/15 ground beef is used in this recipe, but you can change it out with ground turkey or chicken. Try "Beyond Beef," a plant-based ground beef substitute stored in a refrigerator instead of frozen that cooks up well in Sloppy Joes, if you want a vegetarian variant.

Hot Dog: Pay homage to the humble beginnings of the Shack by topping with your Sloppy Joe Mix your all-beef hot dog. You want to slather your bun in Shake Shack Sauce too, of course.

Recipe 5 - Olive Garden's Alfredo Fettuccine

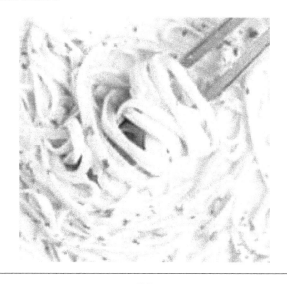

Prep time 5 mins
Cook time 15 mins
Total time 20 mins
Servings 6

Ingredients
Butter high quality, 6 tbsp.
Garlic, minced, 1 tbsp.
All-purpose flour, two tablespoons
Heavy cream, 1.5 cups
1.5 cups of milk, could be of any type
1/2 cup Parmesan cheese, crushed and at ambient temperature
1/2 cup Romano cheese, crushed and at ambient temperature
Salt and black, to taste
1 lb. Fettuccine
Parsley, to garnish

Directions
- Boil the fettuccine as instructed on the box. As the water preheats, the sauce begins to cook.
- Melt butter over medium heat into a large saucepan. Stir in the garlic and cook for 1 minute.
- Whisk the flour inside. Slowly add the heavy cream, then the milk, and whisk continuously.
- Reduce heat to low once the sauce starts bubbling. As it cooks, it will keep on thickening.
- Sprinkle slowly in the cheeses, and continue whisking.
- Drain the pasta and add it carefully until well blended into the sauce. The pasta consumes the sauce, and it gets even thicker.

- Add chopped parsley for garnish, and serve!

Note: You may be compelled to put in more cheese to the sauce to thicken it, but it keeps thickening on standing and even when added to the pasta.

Alfredo sauce is generally thinner than you might think, and you may make it too rich while thickening it further.

For pasta, that is Saucier: 3/4 lb. Pasta can be used instead of a full pound.

Reheating the Alfredo Sauce

- Alfredo sauce can thicken and harden as it cools, but on top of the stove, it can be quickly reheated or microwaved gradually. You'll see it would start taking on more of its original shape as it heats up again.
- Before heating, frozen Alfredo sauce should be thawed in the fridge overnight.
- When done with reheating, add a splash of milk or chicken broth to smooth out if the sauce is too thick.

Macro-nutrients

Calories: 624 kcal, Carbohydrate: 62 g, Protein: 20 g, Fat: 33 g, Saturated Fat: 20 g, Cholesterol: 153 mg, Sodium: 399 mg, Potassium: 357 mg, Fiber: 3 g, Sugar: 2 g, Vitamin A: 925IU, Vitamin C: 2 mg, Calcium: 347 mg, Iron: 2 mg.

Chapter 3: Copycat Recipes- Side Dishes, Salads and Drinks

3.1 Copycat Recipes for side dishes

Recipe 1 - Copycat Cilantro Lime Rice from Chipotle

Chipotle Copycat Cilantro Lime Rice is an easy-to-do recipe that will become a staple in your house. It is beautifully soft and sticky, with a sweet, nutty fragrance. It has sprinkled fresh cilantro throughout, and a vibrant citrus flavor makes this an amazing side dish you are going to make over and over again!

Prep time 5 mins
Cook time 20 mins
Servings 4

Utensils required

Bowl and a saucepan

Ingredients
1 cup of long grain basmati rice
2 Cups of chicken or vegetable stock
Two tsp. of olive oil
Salt, a pinch
(Extra) 1 Tablespoon butter, strongly recommended
3 Tablespoon freshly squeezed lime juice
One lime zest
A cup of finely chopped cilantro leaves

Directions
- **Rinse the rice:** Rinse rice before cooking. It helps eliminate excess starch (surface strand prevents it from sticking together.)
- Place rice in a fine-mesh strainer or a bowl and rinse many times. Gently clean with fingertips by scrubbing rice.
- **Sauté:** Another move to be followed to cook rice perfectly with separate grains. Heat a small amount of oil (olive oil or canola). Sauté rinsed rice in a medium heat pan on the strong bottom sauce. Stir till the rice starts to brown. This phase ensures that rice is cooked correctly and that every grain remains separate.
- **Note:** There is another advantage of lightly frying rice in oil. If you follow this move, rice isn't going to stick down.
- **Water to Rice Ratio:** Add 2 cups of liquid to each 1 cup of long-grain rice. After the rice has been sautéed, add the liquid of your choosing – water or stock of chicken

to bring more flavors. Use vegetable stock for vegetarian choice.
- Scrape rice which sticks into the liquid to the side of the pan.
- **Simmer and Cook:** Simmer to medium-low heat with flame and bring water to boil.
- **Pro-Tip:** Cooking rice at proper temperatures is critical. When cooked at high heat, water can evaporate very easily, preventing the liquids from being absorbed by the rice, so your rice won't be prepared as you wish.
- Cook uncovered until the level of water drops below the rice surface. Then bring down to low flame. Now cover the pan with lid (when approximately 90 percent of water is absorbed and cook for about 12 minutes to simmer.)
- **Note:** Heat should be at the lowest temperature. Otherwise, rice at the bottom will start burning.
- Do not mix in water. Leave it untouched.
- **Let it rest:** Remove the saucepan from the heat until cooked and let it sit without interruption for 5 to 10 minutes. Do not open the lid. It helps to cook the rice through. Rice retains moisture from the steam and makes it nice and fluffy.
- **Flavor:** Open the cap. Add butter, lime juice, cilantro, lime zest, and fluff it gently with a fork or spatula. Apply salt according to taste, if appropriate.
- Serve.

Notes
- For better results, use long grain rice. Wouldn't recommend sticky rice varieties.

- Rinse rice, always. That helps to get rid of excess starch and separates rice.
- **Note:** (to rinse or not to rinse you decide) – Rinsing removes not only excess starch but also cleans any rice dust or debris. If you don't want to rinse rice, go ahead, but remember that your cilantro rice will turn into sticky rice, and if you don't care about sticky rice, you are nice!
- Use chicken broth (or vegetable stock) instead of plain water to add more flavors to rice.
- Lightly frying the rice in oil first helps bring out rice flavors (long-grain rice is aromatic and full of flavors) plus prevents rice from sticking to the bottom of the pan.
- Start with a 1:2 ratio. The entire time, it works well. In case if the rate doesn't work for you, the next time you cook 1 3/4 cup instead of 2 cups for each 1 cup long-grain rice, reduce the water level.
- Cook and simmer heat to low for perfectly cooked rice. Rice retains much of the steam's temperature and cooks well.
- Once cooking is finished, allow the rice to rest, without opening the lid.

Nutritional Data – Please note that the nutritional information given is just a rough approximation and can differ considerably depending on the items and brands used.

Calories: 259 kcal, Carbohydrates: 42 g, Protein: 6 g, Fat: 7 g, Saturated fat: 3 g, Cholesterol: 11 mg, Sodium: 21 mg, Potassium: 213 mg, Fiber: 1 g, Sugar: 2 g, Vitamin A: 357IU, Vitamin C: 5 mg, Calcium: 19 mg, Iron: 1 mg

Recipe 2 - Copycat Longhorn Steakhouse Wild West Shrimp

Prep time 15 mins
Cook time 10 mins
Additional time 5 mins
Yield: 30 pieces

Ingredients
Frying oil (peanut oil can be used)
12 oz. medium, peeled and deveined shrimp
1 cup of flour, self-rising
1/2 cup of cherry peppers (the ones in a jar can be used)
1/4 cup butter
One lemon Juice
Ranch dressing, to dip

Longhorn Prairie Dust (Don't use all the prairie dust)

1/2 cup paprika
Kosher salt, ¼ cup
1/4 cup brown sugar
2 tbsp. of mustard, ground
1/2 cup chili powder
Cumin 1/4 cup, ground
Black pepper, 2 tbsp
1/4 cup garlic, granulated
2 tbsp. cayenne pepper

Directions
- Heat up to 1-inch oil at medium heat. Include a pinch of salt and pepper to the cup of flour in a medium bowl. Dredge shrimp and cook for around 2 minutes or until golden brown color. Take out with a slotted spoon and drain on paper towels. Shift to the tray.
- Melt butter over medium-high heat in another skillet. Add lemon juice and peppers and cook for 5 minutes. Sprinkle lightly with Prairie Dust mixture (you won't need all of it) and pour over shrimp.

Prairie Dust
- Mix all the ingredients of the prairie dust. Store in a covered container. Note: Sprinkle the dust gently on the mixture of shrimps. Do not use it all. Store the leftover Prairie Dust in a covered container.
- Use ranch dressing to serve.

Nutrition Figures
Yield 4
3 oz Serving Size

Amount per Serving: Calories 598, Total Fat 27g, Saturated Fat 10g, Trans Fat 1g, Unsaturated Fat 16g, Cholesterol 212mg, Carbohydrates 67g, Fiber 16g, Protein 31 g

Recipe 3 - Rudy's Creamed Corns

A copycat Rudy's Creamed Corn version, this recipe is great any time of year. This recipe is easy to make and packs in this creamy concoction a lot of flavors.

5 minutes- Prepare Time
3 Hours- Cooking Time
3 hours, 5 mins- Total Time

Ingredients
16 oz. fully frozen kernel corn
6 oz cream cheese, cubed (Note: if you're trying to save calories, you can use low fat)
1/2 cup heavy cream, whipping
2 tbsp of sugar

Four tablespoons of unsalted butter
Black pepper, fresh and ground
1/2 tsp salt

Directions
- Place the corn on the bottom, using a crockpot.
- Layer over cream cheese, whipping cream, and sugar.
- Dice the butter and stir in the mixture.
- Season with pepper and salt. Combine to blend.
- Cover and simmer for 3 hours at low heat until smooth, stirring occasionally.

Nutrition

Calories 330, Fat 18.38 g, Carbs 32.07g, Protein 5.71 g

Recipe 4 - Chili's Black Beans

Prep time 10 mins
Cook time 25 mins

Total time 35 mins
Servings: 1

Ingredients
31 ounces 2 cans black beans
1/2 tsp. of sugar
1/2 tsp. of chili powder
1/2 tsp. of garlic powder

Instructions
- In a saucepan, put the black beans, sugar, chili powder, and garlic powder and mix through.
- Let it simmer for around 20-25 minutes at low heat.
- Remove from heat and put in a bowl, or serve with meat or fish, your choice.

Tips for this recipe
- If you are using dry black beans, give more time. See the Instructions above.
- Serve the black beans with a few tortilla chips. Or with some chicken, Pico de Gallo, and rice. Place beans onto the plate top. They will cover the plate center. Place chicken breast in the middle, with your rice serving on the side, a generous Pico de Gallo. And add a tbsp of crushed tortilla chips.

Nutrition
Calories: 1175 kcal, Carbohydrate: 211 g, Protein: 78 g, Fat: 4 g, Saturated fat: 1 g, Cholesterol: 0 mg, Sodium: 26 mg, Potassium: 3119 mg, Fiber: 76 g, Sugar: 2 g, Vitamin A: 350IU, Calcium: 237 mg, Iron: 18.5 mg

3.2 Copycat Salad Recipes

Recipe 1 - Applebee's Oriental Chicken Salad

Prep time 20 mins
Total time 20 mins
Servings: 4

Ingredients

Salad
5 cups of romaine lettuce, chopped-around one head
1 1/2 cups of shredded red cabbage
1 1/2 cup carrots, shredded
Crispy Asian Chicken Tenders, 8

1/3 cup cut, toasted almonds
Chow Mein noodles 1/3 cup
2 Green Onions-Cut

Dressing
1/2 cup plain Greek yogurt
Honey, 2 tbsp.
1 tbsp. of rice vinegar
2 Dijon Mustard teaspoons
1/4 tsp. sesame oil
1/8 tsp. of kosher salt
1-2 tablespoonful of non-fat milk-if required

Directions
- **Prepare the dressing:** Mix the Greek yogurt, butter, vinegar, mustard, sesame oil, and salt in a small bowl or large measuring cup. Taste and add salt as you wish. Add 1 to 2 tablespoons of milk until the perfect consistency is achieved if the dressing is too thick for your taste.
- Toss the romaine, red cabbage, and carrots into a large mixing bowl. Arrange on top the chicken tenders. Drizzle the dressing on top. Sprinkle with the noodles, almonds, and green onions. Enjoy it straight away.

Nutrition
Calories: 370, Fat: 11 g, Cholesterol: 106 mg, Sodium: 304 mg, Carbohydrate: 42 g, Fiber: 6 g, Sugar: 16 g, Protein: 29 g

Recipe 2 - Mediterranean Kale Salad- copycat from Panera Bread

A copycat for the wonderful Panera Bread Modern Greek Salad with chicken, this Mediterranean kale and quinoa salad is so smooth and satisfying!

Prep time 15 mins
Cook time 15 mins
Servings: 2

Ingredients

4 cups, sliced with a knife, curly green kale
1/4 tsp. of salt
1/4 teaspoon of freshly cracked pepper
1 1/2 cups of prepared chicken, cut into pieces
1/2 cup of cooked quinoa
1 cup of cherry tomatoes, half cut
1/2 cup roasted red pepper, chopped
Thinly sliced 1/2 cup cucumber
1/3 cup of Kalamata olives, diced
Sliced almonds: 1/4 cup
1/4 cup of feta crumbled cheese
2 tbsp. of shallot, sliced
Lemon wedges

Lemon Vinaigrette
Red wine vinegar, ¼ cup
3 tbsp. of lemon juice
1 1/2 tbsp. of honey
Two cloves of garlic, nicely cut or pressed
Dill weed, a half teaspoon
Oregano dried 1/4 teaspoon
1/4 tsp. salt
1/4 tsp. pepper
Extra virgin olive oil, ½ cup

Directions
- Cook your quinoa, as required, according to the directions of the package. It will take roughly fifteen minutes!

- Place the kale in a bowl and apply one teaspoon of olive oil to the leaves. Place for 10 minutes aside. Season it with salt and pepper after 1 minute, and toss again.
- Add the chicken and quinoa to the kale bowl to assemble the salad, and toss again. Tomatoes, all the given peppers, cucumber, olives, almonds, feta, and shallot are to be included. Drizzle the dressing on and mix. Serve with extra dressing and a slice of lemon.

Lemon Vinaigrette
Whisk the vinegar, lemon juice, sugar, garlic, dill, oregano, salt, and pepper together in a cup. Keep whisking while pouring in the olive oil. This dressing stays good in the refrigerator in a sealed jar for about a week, so feel easy to prepare a double batch if you wish.

Nutrition
390 Calories, Fat 36 g, Carbs 11 g, Fiber 4 g, Protein 6 g

3.3 Copycat Drink Recipes

Recipe 1 - Chick-Fil-A Frosted Lemonade (copycat)

Copycat Recipe Chick-fil-A Frosted Lemonade is a quick low-carb, keto recipe that provides the ideal healthy alternative to this famous frozen drink. This milkshake is made with freshly pressed lemons, vanilla ice cream with no-sugar-added, and you can top it with whipped cream. Ditch the calories and extra carbs for this slim, homemade version.

Prep time 10 mins
Servings: 2

Ingredients
(Juice of) Two lemons
2 cups of vanilla ice cream
Ice-2 cups
2-3 tablespoons Sweetener (Confectioner's). Start with two sweetener spoons and change to your desired taste. 3 Tablespoons or above are more in accordance with the sweetness of the drink at Chick-fil-A.

Directions
- Add all the ingredients into a mixer.
- Mix. Combine. You may use the ice-cream feature on your high-powered Instant Pot blender. This would result in a blend time of 1 minute and 25 seconds. Use your decision on what speed and timing your blender would work best at. Mix until the mixture becomes dense and creamy. The blend shouldn't be runny.
- Pour into the cups or glasses and enjoy!

Notes
- Macros are measured using Vanilla ice cream from Rebel Low-Carb High Fat. Choose an ice cream brand that aligns with your macro objectives, if you want less fat.
- Less lemon can be used to reduce net carbs. By using one lemon instead of 2, net carbs would be reduced to 6 per drink.
- Confectioner's sweetener is used to prevent the taste of crystals/grains instead of granular ones.

Nutrition
Calories: 322 kcal, Hydrocarbons: 9 g, Proteins: 9 g, Fat: 34 g

Recipe 2 - Starbuck's Pumpkin Spice Latte

Are you using lattes with pumpkin spice? Here's a homemade copycat recipe for you. This mixture yields a 16 oz drink.
Prep time 10 mins
Total time 10 mins

Ingredients
Two tablespoonful of pumpkin puree
Two tablespoons of condensed milk, sweetened
1/2 teaspoonful of pumpkin pie spice, and more for topping
1 cup of milk
1 cup of coffee, with a good brew
One-fourth cup whipped cream

Directions
- To mix ingredients, add pumpkin, sweetened condensed milk, pumpkin pie spice, and milk to a pan and heat over medium-low whisking to blend the ingredients.

- When the mixture starts bubbling, add the coffee and raise heat to simmer.
- Continue whisking until steamy and hot.
- Pour over with whipped cream and extra pumpkin pie spice into a mug.

Notes

If you want extra sugar in your latte, increase the sweetened condensed milk to 1/4 cup. You can make it taste less sweet than a standard Starbucks PSL using the two tablespoons mentioned.

Nutrition

Sum per Serving: Calories: 302, Total Fat: 12g, Saturated fat: 7g, Trans fat: 0g, Unsaturated fat: 4g, Cholesterol: 44mg, Sodium: 184mg, Carbohydrates: 1g, Sugar: 23g, Protein: 13g

Recipe 3 - Mocha Frappe McDonald's

Prep time 1 hour
Servings: 5

Ingredients
2 cups coffee, cold
2 Cups of unsweetened almond milk (or dairy regular milk)
3 1/2 tbsp. of chocolate syrup
3 1/2 tbsp. of granulated sugar
Whipped cream, to garnish
Chocolate syrup, extra for garnish
Grated chocolate bar, to garnish

Directions
- Infuse the coffee and let it cool down to near room temperature.
- Pour coffee carefully into ice cube trays, and freeze.
- For mixing, add frozen coffee sticks, almond milk, chocolate syrup, and sugar.
- Blend until it reaches the desired texture.
- Finish with whipped cream, chocolate syrup drizzle, and if you prefer, shaved chocolate.

Coffee, frozen
Oh yeah, it's good. Only brew some of your favorite coffee and let it cool down to room temperature (or even decaf if you prefer). Pour the chilled coffee into ice cube trays and pop them up until frozen in the fridge.

So maybe you'd think, why can't you just use standard coffee and add ice cubes? Okay. But as the ice melts, your drink will be watered down! So you get the frozen component by freezing the coffee into ice cubes to make it nice, icy, and chilled but without diluting your drink!

Some variations
Dairy – Almond milk has been used to develop this recipe. However, you can also transform this recipe using soy milk, regular dairy milk, and a half and half (a half-milk and half-cream American dairy product).

Reduced sugar – Some readers may wonder whether the sugar-free or reduced sugar items could be used to produce this recipe. And yes, sure they could be! A better alternative to regular syrup is the sugar-free chocolate syrup. And alternatives to sugar may be used instead of the granulated sugar. Alternatively, you can remove the granulated sugar-it's just a matter of taste and how sweet you like stuff.

Other Varieties – Certain syrup varieties can be used instead of regular chocolate if you would like. Torani, as does Ghirardelli, makes some fantastic syrups. Different flavors could be sugar, and maple syrup salted chocolate!
The mint is suitable as a garnish, but to make this a holiday peppermint mocha drink, you could add some peppermint extract!

Making Mocha Frappes before time
As this is a frozen drink, this is a recipe that is best prepared before serving. You should do the first part of this recipe in advance, however. Brew the coffee and let it cool down (or use coffee leftover). Pour over ice cube trays and freeze until solid and frozen. In a freezer bag, add the cubes and freeze for up to 2 months.

Storage
Leftovers can be placed in a container that is safe and frozen for up to a month — Thaw before making a drink.

Special utensils and equipment for this recipe

Blender – You can usually use the blender when you make this recipe. It has got high power, and it does not break the bank.

Torani Syrups – These can be found in your grocery store; you just can see all the choices.

Ghirardelli Syrups – Not as many Torani varieties are there but great taste.

Nutritional facts
510 Calories, Fat 20 g, Carbs 73 g, Fiber 1 g, Protein 8 g

Chapter 4: Hamburgers and desserts

4.1 Copycat Hamburger Recipes

Recipe 1 - Burger King Whooper

The basic Whopper consists of only eight simple ingredients. However, as the famous slogan of Burger King suggests, with different variations and inclusions, such as American cheese, pork, mustard, guacamole, or jalapeño peppers, you can "have it your way" (since modified to "be your way"). If "your way" is vegetarian, you'll even be made a veggie Whopper.

In 2009 Burger King started selling the Whopper Bar, which the company described as a more "playful" variation on the Burger King standard. A Whopper Bar features an open kitchen with a semi-circular metal countertop. Customers can sit down on a barstool and enjoy watching their food being cooked. For your simple Whopper Burger, Whopper Bars have loads of different Whopper toppings – bacon, guacamole, crispy onions, BBQ sauce, and more. Whopper bars can be found in shopping malls, airports, casinos, and similar areas. When your plane is delayed, enjoying a Whopper in a Whopper Bar will help keep your frustration down.

The baseline Whopper is 1/4 lb. Juicy grilled beef topped with fresh tomatoes and lettuce, creamy mayonnaise, tangy ketchup, crunchy pickles, and sliced white onions on a soft bun of sesame seeds. The given simple recipe for Whopper will allow you to make a Whopper at home with ease. Should not have a mini-Whopper-bar party at the backyard on special occasions? Consider the fun you would have while grilling outdoors. Offer a variety of options for your family and guests to have their way through their Whopper. Here's the basic recipe with which you can enjoy Whoppers during the whole summer.

Prep time 10 mins
Cook time 10 mins
Total time 20 mins
Servings: 4

Ingredients
1 pound ground beef
1/2 teaspoon of salt

1/4 tsp. black pepper
4 Hamburger buns with sesame
12 slices of pickles
Ketchup: 4 tablespoons
Mayonnaise: 4 tbsp.
1/2 white onion, sliced

Directions
- Put salt and pepper on the ground beef and shape into patties. In a skillet, butter hamburger buns and toast until lightly browned, and put aside. Heat a grill over medium to high heat. Cook the burger on each side for two to three minutes, and add a dash of salt to the hamburger when cooking.
- Make the burger by putting the meat on the bottom bun, then add 3 or 4 slices of dill pickle, 3 or 4 slices of ringed onion, 2 or 3 slices of tomato. Then squirt a small amount of ketchup over the burger, add the lettuce, then spread the mayonnaise over the top bun and put the top bun on the burger.

Macro Nutrients
Calories: 526 kcal, Carbohydrates: 27 g, Protein: 24 g, Fat: 34 g, Saturated fat: 10 g, Cholesterol: 86 mg, Sodium: 988 mg, Potassium: 446 mg, Fiber: 1 g, Sugar: 7 g, Vitamin A: 115IU, Vitamin C: 2.1 mg, Calcium: 106 mg, Iron: 3.8 mg

Recipe 2 - Burger King-BK Big Fish Copycat

Prep and cook time 20 mins
Servings: 1

Ingredients
1 Cod fillet (approx. 3.5 oz)
1 White from Egg
1 tsp. milk
All-purpose flour, 1 Teaspoon
1 Tablespoon of fine, dry breadcrumbs
Season with salt, one pinch
Hamburgers buns, 1
1 Slice of American cheese
1/2 cup iceberg lettuce, shredded
One tablespoon tartar sauce (* BK tartar sauce ingredients and method at the end of the directions)
Cooking spray flavored with olive oil

Directions
- Beat the egg white along with the milk until well blended.
- Mix the salt and flour in a separate dish. Blend well.
- Dip the fish into the mixture of the flour, then the mixture of the eggs and the bread's crumbs. Make sure the fish is entirely and evenly coated by them all.
- Lightly spray olive oil on a non-stick baking sheet. Throw the fish onto the baking sheet.
- It should be baked for about 7 minutes (or until the breading is crisp) in a 450 ° preheated oven. Flip the fish and bake for 5-7 minutes more.
- Meanwhile, the hamburger bun is toasted in a preheated skillet.
- Put a bun on a plate at the bottom. Top with the sauce, fish, cheese, and lettuce. Flip the sandwich bun onto the top. And voila, really delicious meal ready!

BK Tartar Sauce-In, a bowl, mix 1/4 cup mayonnaise, two tablespoons of dill pickle relish and two teaspoons of corn syrup. Shake well. This should be about 1/3 cup tartar sauce and can be cooled in an airtight container for up to a month.

Nutrients
Calories 417.6, Fats 68 g, Cholesterol 109.1 mg, Carbs 30.8 g, Sodium 733.2 mg, Fiber 1.7 g, Sugars 4.1 g

Recipe 3 - Copycat McDonald's Big Mac

Prep time 10 mins
Cook time 20 mins
Additional time 8 hours
Total time 8 hours 30 mins
Yield: 6 Big Macs

Ingredients

Sauce
Mayo: ½ cup
French dressing: 2 tbsp.
Sweet relish: 1 tbsp.
Dill pickle juice: 3 tbsp
1 Teaspoon of sugar
One teaspoon of dried onion, minced
Ketchup 1 teaspoon
Salt, a dash

Burgers

2 Lbs. of lean ground beef, shaped into 12 large thin patties
Salt and Pepper
12 Hamburger buns with sesame seeds, six tops, and 12 bottoms
Butter
Chopped lettuce
Dill pickles
Onions, minced
American sliced cheese

Instructions

- **To make the sauce:** mix all the ingredients and cover and refrigerate for 24 hours.
- Fry the burgers until done in one skillet. Salt and pepper the patties and fry. Top with slices of American cheese, heat until melted.
- Butter the insides of the buns in another pan, and toast over medium-high heat. (Like a grilled cheese). Place aside.
- Put the sauce on each bun's buttered side, put the onions, pickles, and lettuce on the bottom and the middle. Put the top of the burger. Place them aside.
- Serve hot with fries at the side.

Macro-Nutrients

Calories: 887, Total fat: 68 g, Saturated fat: 16g, Trans fat: 1g, Unsaturated fat: 46g, Cholesterol: 142mg, Sodium: 656mg, Carbs: 24g, Fiber: 9g, Sugar: 5g, Protein: 49g

4.2 Copycat Dessert Recipes

Recipe 1 - Cracker Barrel Coca Cola Cake

Some people may find it strange that this recipe for chocolate cake includes Coca-Cola, which might sound weird. Yet try it out, and you will never go anywhere else! It just makes the typical chocolate cake a little more unique.

Prep time 20 mins
Cook time 30 mins
Servings: 10

Ingredients
Coca-Cola, 1 cup
Vegetable oil, ½ cup
Salted butter, ½ cup
Unsweetened Cocoa Powder, 1/3 cup

Sugar, 2 cups
All-purpose flour, 2 cups
Eggs, 2
1/2 cup buttermilk
1 tsp baking soda
2 tsp vanilla extract

For the frosting
1/4 cup unsweetened cocoa powder
1/2 cup (1 stick) salted butter
1/4 cup Coca-Cola
3 cups powdered sugar
1 tsp vanilla extract

Directions
- Set the oven to 350 degrees F temperature. Butter and flour a 13x9 pan for cake. Set away.
- In a large, deep utensil, mix sugar and flour. Set aside.
- In a saucepan, boil the butter, Coca Cola, vegetable oil, and unsweetened cocoa.
- Pour into the flour mixture and beat on medium-low for about one minute. Include eggs, buttermilk, baking soda, and vanilla and beat for another minute on medium speed.
- Layer the batter into the 13x9 prepared cake tray. Bake for around 30 minutes duration or until a fork or a knife, when inserted, appears clean from the middle of the cake.
- Prepare the frosting. In a pan over medium heat, put the butter, cocoa powder, and Coca Cola to boil. Remove

from heat and add the icing sugar and vanilla. Pour over cake and spread easily.
- Allow the cake to cool.
- Serve with vanilla ice cream and enjoy!

Notes

- You can also include 1/4 cup chocolate syrup or sauce and 1/2 cup chopped pecans to the frosting. Simply add as you whisk in the powdered sugar and vanilla. Or simply pour the chocolate syrup over the vanilla ice cream!

Nutrition
Calories 747.5, fats 296 g, Cholesterol 47.7 mg, Sodium 435.4 mg, Carbs 110.4 g, Fiber 1.8 g, Sugar 87.5 g, Proteins 5.7 g

Recipe 2 - Trader Joe's Gone Bananas

Prep time 10 mins
Servings: 2

Ingredients
Banana: 1
1 cup of dark chocolate or chocolate chips
Coconut oil: 2 tbsp

Directions
- Slice the banana onto a tray and put the slices in. Shift the platter in the freezer until the frozen bananas are firm for an hour.
- In the meantime, place the chocolate chips and coconut oil in a tiny safe bowl or measuring cup. Microwave and then stir for 30 seconds. Microwave and stir again for another 15 seconds until all the chocolate is melted and smooth. If need be, put it back in the microwave for a few seconds. Don't have to overheat. Set aside the chocolate to cool off.
- Dip them in the cooled chocolate when the bananas are frozen, then paint on all sides. You can practice putting the slices on a fork, and then using a spoon to help drizzle the chocolate around. Let any excess chocolate fall apart before setting the slice on waxed paper or parchment paper. Put the slices straight back into the freezer.
- The slices can be stored in a freezer baggie with a ziplock once the chocolate has hardened.

Make them your way.

- Cover the frozen bananas with a dab of peanut butter before covering them, if you prefer.
- Slide a stick used for popsicles into the sliced bananas before freezing and dipping.

Macro-nutrients
Calories 100, Fat 3.5 g, Carbs 16 g, Protein 1 g

Recipe 3 - Ben and Jerry's Cherry Garcia Ice cream

Makes eight servings

Ingredients
1-pint whipping cream, heavy
 One can of 15 ounces of condensed milk, sweetened

Chocolate chunks, 1 cup
Fresh cherries, cut in half and pitted, 1 ½ cups
One teaspoon of vanilla extract

Directions
- Beat the heavy cream in a stand mixer until the peaks become prominent.
- Fold in the sweetened condensed milk, chocolate chunks, cherries, and vanilla once the stiff peaks have formed.
- Freeze the ice cream in a bread loaf pan until it has set.

Calories
For Serving Size: 1: Calories: 615, Sugar: 60, Fat: 36, Saturated fat: 23, Unsaturated fat: 8, Trans fat: 0, Carbohydrate: 65, Fiber: 3, Protein: 9

Chapter 5: Special Bonus Artisan bread

5.1 Artisan Bread Recipes

Recipe 1 - No-Knead Crusty Artisan Bread

Yield: 1 loaf

Ingredients
All-purpose flour 3 cups

Kosher salt two teaspoons (not table salt)
1/2 teaspoon of dry yeast (active or highly active dry works well)
1 1/2 cups of water, lukewarm
Special kitchen utensils needed: Dutch oven or large oven-safe dish/bowl and lid *

Directions
- Stir the flour, salt, and leaven together in a large bowl. Use a wooden spoon to stir in water until the mixture forms a cohesive but shaggy dough. Don't overwork your dough. The less you "work" it, the softer the flaccid air pockets will form.
- The bowl should be tightly covered with plastic wrap. Let the dough sit for 8–24 hours at room temperature *. The dough is about to bubble and rise.
- Set oven temperature to 450 degrees F once the dough is ready. Place your uncovered Dutch oven for 30 minutes in the preheated oven.
- Turn the dough onto a well-floured surface while your Dutch oven preheats. Form the dough into a ball with floured hands. Broadly cover the dough with plastic wrap, and let rest.
- Remove the Dutch oven carefully after the 30 minutes are up. Place the bread dough inside with floured hands. (If your Dutch oven is not enamel-coated, you can put parchment under the dough.)
- Replace cover and bake over covered for 30 minutes. Carefully remove the cover and bake, uncovered, for 7-15 minutes more.

- Remove bread carefully to a cutting board and slice with a knife for bread.
- Enjoy it!

Notes
- The time to bake uncovered depends on your oven. The bread in some ovens only needs to be uncovered for 7 minutes, until it is crispy and golden brown, but this can vary. Just stick to it!
- Setting the Dutch oven at 450 degrees F isn't going to damage it or the top knob.
- You may let the dough rise anywhere between 8-24 hours, and it will beautifully bake up. Just make sure it has risen to the surface and appears to be "bubbling."
- The Dutch oven/baking dish/pot needs not to be greased. The bread usually would not get stuck to the pot. Put a segment of parchment paper under your dough before placing it in your container if you're concerned.
- It is not recommended using whole wheat flour or white whole wheat flour as part of this recipe. The out coming bread will be very dense, and not as delicious and fluffy.
- Le Creuset's 5.5 quarter cast iron pot has been used here, but you can use any large oven-safe dish and cover. All of these work as well: a baking dish covered with aluminum foil, crockpot inserted, stainless steel pot with a cover, pizza stone with an oven-safe bowl to cover the bread, and old cast iron Dutch oven.

- Add any mix-ins you like-all work well with herbs, spices, dried fruit, chopped nuts, and cheese. It is endorsed that they are added to the initial flour-yeast mixture so as not to overwork the mix-ins into the dough. The less you "work" it, the softer, flabby air pockets you encourage to form!

Recipe 2- Four ingredient easy Artisan Bread

Prep time 5 mins
Cook time 45 mins
Resting time 8 hours
Total time 50 mins
Servings: 12 slices

Ingredients
Three cups of all-purpose flour
One tsp. of salt
1/2 teaspoon of yeast
Warm water, 1.5 cups

Directions
- Stir up the flour, salt, yeast, and water in a bowl until mixed. Seal with plastic wrapping and let rest for 8-24 hours at room temperature.
- Take the dough out onto a floured countertop, forming a ball. (Place it on parchment paper if you wish.)
- Rest for about 30 minutes. Place a safe baking dish with high sides in the oven and preheat to 450 degrees Celsius.
- Slash an "X" over the bread. Transfer carefully to a baking dish and cover. (If you use parchment paper, you can pick up the edges of the paper and put the dough and the paper together in the baking platter.)
- Bake for about thirty minutes, covered. Take the cover off and bake for about 15 minutes, until the bread is quite a golden brown.
- Before slicing, cool.

Conclusion

All the ingredients and guidelines provided in this book, if followed carefully, might help produce accurate versions of the replicated recipes at home. Nevertheless, variations may always be brought about in the ingredients to create more alternate versions of the given methods. Ben and Jerry's Cherry Gracia Ice-cream, for instance, could be prepared with different flavorings, with the given base ingredients. The quantities may be varied likewise, depending upon the serving size and requirement. However, the estimated calories, macro-nutrients, and the dishes' final looks may come out different from the ones given inside the book. All the temperatures mentioned are for the best of the results. Any variations in the given temperatures may or may not produce the same results.